Georgia Bulldogs Football Quiz Book

Chris Bradshaw

For rights and permissions, please contact:

Chris Bradshaw

C_D_Bradshaw@hotmail.com

ISBN: 1-9161230-9-0
ISBN-13: 978-1-9161230-9-0

Front cover image created by headfuzz by grimboid. Check out his great collection of TV, movie and sport-themed posters online at:

https://www.etsy.com/shop/headfuzzbygrimboid

Introduction

Think you know about the Georgia Bulldogs? Put your knowledge to the test with this collection of quizzes on all things red and black.

The book covers the whole history of the Bulldogs, from the school's earliest days, the glory years under Vince Dooley, right up to the 2021 National Champions.

The biggest names in UGA's history are present and correct so look out for questions on Herschel Walker, David Greene, Todd Gurley, David Pollack, Champ Bailey, Brock Bowers, Stetson Bennett and many more.

There are 500 questions in all covering running backs and receivers, coaches and quarterbacks, pass rushers and punters and much else besides.

Each quiz contains a selection of 20 questions and is either a mixed bag of pot luck testers or is centered on a specific category such as the the 1980 National Champions or defense.

There are easy, medium and hard questions offering something for Georgia greenhorns as well as professors of Bulldogs history.

You'll find the answers to each quiz at the bottom of the following quiz. For example, the answers to Quiz 1: Pot Luck, are underneath Quiz 2: College Football Championship. The only exception is Quiz 25: Anagrams. The answers to these can be found under the Quiz 1 questions.

All records and statistics are accurate up to the close of the 2022 season and relate to the regular season only (excluding Bowl Games) unless otherwise stated.

We hope you enjoy the Georgia Bulldogs Football Quiz Book.

May 2023 Update

This latest edition of the Georgia Bulldogs Trivia Quiz Book has been fully revised and updated. All statistics and records are now accurate to the start of the 2023 season.

You'll also find 60 brand-new trivia teasers to test your knowledge on all things Dawgs, including sets on the 2022 National Championship team and the College Football Championship Final. These are at the back of the book in the Bonus Questions section. As usual, you'll find the answers to each quiz at the bottom of the quiz that follows.

Good luck!

About the Author

Chris Bradshaw has written more than 20 quiz books including titles for Britain's biggest selling daily newspaper, The Sun, and The Times (of London). In addition to college football, he has written extensively on the NFL, soccer, cricket, darts and poker.

He lives in Birmingham, England and has been following football for over 30 years.

Acknowledgements

Many thanks to Ken and Veronica Bradshaw, Heidi Grant, Steph, James, Ben and Will Roe and Graham Nash.

CONTENTS

Bonus Questions

Quiz 1: Pot Luck

1. Which head coach steered the 2021 and 2022 Bulldogs to the National Championship?

2. What color is the Bulldogs' helmet?

3. What is the name of the Bulldogs' famous fight song?

4. Did the Bulldogs win the 2021/22 National Championship Game wearing home or road uniforms?

5. Which Bulldog was the winner of 2021 Butkus Award which is given to the nation's outstanding linebacker?

6. Which running back threw an 18-yard TD pass in the 2021 College Championship semifinal?

7. Who caught that famous trick play pass?

8. The National Championship Game is usually held on what day of the week?

9. Which offensive star was named 2021's SEC Freshman of the Year?

10. Georgia's rivalry with which opponent is known as 'Clean, Old-Fashioned Hate'?

11. Who scored a famous 93-yard go-ahead touchdown in a November 1980 win over Florida?

12. Which former Bulldog was a member of the US bobsleigh team at the 1992 Winter Olympic Games?

13. In what year did Vince Dooley become UGA's head coach?

14. Who was Vince Dooley describing when he said, 'He's the best defensive player I've ever coached and maybe the best one I've ever seen'?

15. Which defensive star was also holder of the school long jump record, a record that remained intact until February 2021?

16. What number jersey did quarterback Stetson Bennett wear?

17. True or false – Sanford Stadium hosted soccer games at the 1996 Olympics?

18. Which Georgia rusher from the 1910s and member of the College Football Hall of Fame later became a four-time mayor of Athens?

19. What was former Bulldogs quarterback Zeke Bratkowski's given first name? a) Edgar b) Edmund c) Edward

20. In 2017 the Bulldogs set a school record after scoring how many rushing touchdowns? a) 41 b) 42 c) 43

Quiz 25: Answers

1. Dan Lanning 2. Payne 3. 7 TDs 4. Greyson Lambert 5. Kendrell Bell 6. Hines Ward 7. True 8. Zamir White 9. Auburn 10. 24 games 11. Leonard Floyd 12. Losing 13. Jim Donnan 14. Ray Goff 15. Herschel Walker 16. Stetson Bennett 17. Christopher Smith 18. Valdosta State 19. 20. c) $7.13 million

Quiz 2: 2021/22 College Football Championship

1. Which team did the Bulldogs defeat to claim the National Championship?

2. What was the final score in the National Championship Game?

3. The National Championship Game was hosted at which stadium?

4. Who scored Georgia's only rushing touchdown in the National Championship Game?

5. Which two Bulldogs caught touchdown passes?

6. Which senior recorded Georgia's first turnover with a pick early in the third quarter?

7. Did the Bulldogs go into the game as 3-point favorite or a 3-point underdog?

8. True or false – The Bulldogs never trailed throughout the whole of the National Championship Game?

9. Who was named the game's offensive MVP?

10. Which freshman sealed the National Championship victory after returning a pick 79 yards for a score with less than a minute left?

11. Who led the team in receiving yards in the National Championship Game despite registering just a single catch?

12. Who was named the game's defensive MVP?

13. The Bulldogs went into the playoffs as what number seed?

14. Zamir White was one of two Georgia backs with 50+ rushing yards in the National Championship Game. Who was the other?

15. Which defensive lineman blocked a field goal in the third quarter?

16. True or false – The Bulldogs gained fewer yards than their opponent and lost the time of possession battle in the National Championship Game?

17. How many sacks did the Bulldogs register in the Championship Game?

18. Which multiple Grammy nominee sang the national anthem at the Championship Game?

19. How many points did the Bulldogs score in the first half? a) 3 b) 6 c) 9

20. The Bulldogs held their opponent to how many rushing yards? a) 30 b) 60 c) 90

Quiz 1: Answers

1. Kirby Smart 2. Red 3. 'Glory, Glory' 4. Road 5. Nakobe Dean 6. Kenny McIntosh 7. Adonai Mitchell 8. Monday 9. Brock Bowers 10. Georgia Tech 11. Lindsay Scott 12. Herschel Walker 13. 1964 14. Terry Hoage 15. Champ Bailey 16. #13 17. True 18. Bob McWhorter 19. b) Edmund 20. b) 42

Quiz 3: Pot Luck

1. Is the field at Sanford Stadium made of grass or artificial turf?

2. Who was the offensive coordinator on the 2021 and 2022 National Championship teams?

3. What is the name of the band that plays at Bulldogs home games?

4. What color is the G logo on the Bulldogs helmet?

5. The Bulldogs play in which Division of the SEC – Eastern or Western?

6. What are the two teams called in the G-Day Spring Game?

7. Prior to the 2021/22 National Championship triumph, the Bulldogs had lost how many straight games to Alabama?

8. In what year did the Bulldogs play their first game at Sanford Stadium?

9. Which Ivy League opponent did Georgia face in that historic game?

10. Which former Bulldogs defensive star went on to become a successful wine producer?

11. True or false – Vince Dooley is a member of the Sports Hall of Fame in Alabama as well as in Georgia?

12. Which legendary UGA defender was inducted into the College Football Hall of Fame as part of the class of 2020?

13. What number jersey does star tight end Brock Bowers wear?

14. True or false – Stetson Bennett threw at least one touchdown pass during each game of the 2021 National Championship season?

15. In 2021, who became just the second Bulldog to win the Outland Trophy which is awarded to the top interior lineman in college football?

16. What was the seating capacity of Stanford Stadium when it first opened?

17. What was former Bulldogs star Champ Bailey's given first name?

18. Which former Bulldog was named the NFL Offensive Player of the Year in 2017?

19. What is the most times the Bulldogs have punted in a single game? a) 10 b) 12 c) 14

20. What was the legendary Bulldogs coach 'Pop' Warner's given first name? a) George b) Glenn c) Griff

Quiz 2: Answers

1. Alabama 2. Bulldogs 33-18 Crimson Tide 3. Lucas Oil Stadium, Indianapolis 4. Zamir White 5. Adonai Mitchell and Brock Bowers 6. Christopher Smith 7. A 3-point favorite 8. False 9. Stetson Bennett 10. Kelee Ringo 11. George Pickens 12. Lewis Cine 13. Three 14. James Cook 15. Jalen Carter 16. True 17. Four 18. Natalie Grant 19. b) 6 points 20. a) 30 yards

Quiz 4: 2021 National Champions

1. The Bulldogs opened the season with a 10-3 win over which ACC opponent?

2. That season opener was played at which neutral venue?

3. The Bulldogs reached the College Football Championship after defeating which Big 10 school in the semi-final?

4. What was the score in that game?

5. That semi-final was hosted in which city?

6. Who was the only opponent to defeat the Bulldogs during the 2021 season?

7. The Bulldogs routed which conference rival by a score of 62-0 in week 4?

8. With 856 yards, who was Georgia's leading rusher during the 2021 season?

9. Who was the only Bulldog to amass over 1,000 yards from scrimmage during the 2021 season?

10. Who led the team with 13 touchdown receptions in 2021?

11. Which senior linebacker led the team with 6.5 sacks in 2021?

12. Two other Bulldogs, one linebacker and one lineman, each recorded 6 sacks in 2021. Can you name the pair?

13. The Chuck Bednarick Award, which is given to college football's best defensive player, was won in 2021 by which Georgia Bulldog?

14. Who was the only Bulldogs offensive player named to the 2021 All SEC First Team?

15. Which three Bulldogs defenders also received 2021 All SEC First Team recognition?

16. Stetson Bennett led the team with 29 TD passes in 2021. Who was next on that list with seven?

17. Which Georgia QB threw his first career TD pass against the UAB Blazers in September 2021?

18. Whose four interceptions were the most by a Bulldogs defender in 2021?

19. How many points did the Bulldogs score during the 2021 season? a) 559 b) 569 c) 579

20. The Bulldogs started the season ranked in what position on the AP Poll? a) 3rd b) 4th c) 5th

Quiz 3: Answers

1. Grass 2. Todd Monken 3. The Redcoat Band 4. Black 5. Eastern 6. Red and Black 7. Seven games 8. 1929 9. Yale Bulldogs 10. Terry Hoage 11. True 12. David Pollack 13. #19 14. False 15. Jordan Davis 16. 30,000 17. Roland 18. Todd Gurley 19. b) 14 times 20. b) Glenn

Quiz 5: Pot Luck

1. Who was named the Offensive MVP in the 2021/22 National Championship semi-final?

2. Who was the head coach of the 1980 National Championship team?

3. In what year did the Bulldogs last register a losing season?

4. The Heritage Hall is named after which pair of Georgia coaches?

5. What color is the single stripe in the middle of the Bulldogs helmet?

6. In what year did the Bulldogs play their first night game at Sanford Stadium?

7. Georgia shared a 7-7 tie in that maiden floodlit encounter against which opponent?

8. Which receiver's 93-yard touchdown catch at LSU in 2003 is the second longest in team history?

9. Which quarterback threw that 93-yard TD pass?

10. What do the letters JT stand for in the name of quarterback J.T. Daniels?

11. What was the first name of Dr. S.V. Sanford. After whom the Bulldogs' stadium is named?

12. Vince Dooley's last season as the head coach of the Bulldogs was in what year?

13. True or false – When David Greene finished his UGA career he had more wins as a starting quarterback than anyone else in the history of the NCAA?

14. Which Bulldog was named Freshman of the Year 2021 by the Football Writers Association of America?

15. A 2010 episode of the hit TV drama 'Weeds' was named after which former Bulldogs quarterback?

16. The longest pass during the 2021 season was an 89-yard touchdown from Stetson Bennett to which receiver?

17. True or false – Former Bulldogs punter Drew Butler is the son of former Bulldogs kicker Kevin Butler?

18. Herschel Walker tied an NCAA record in 1981 after rushing for 100 yards or more in how many games?

19. By what name is Georgia's fanbase sometimes know? a) Bulldog Country b) Bulldog Nation c) Bulldog World

20. Jack Podlesny set a school record in 2022 after converting how many extra points? a) 71 b) 73 c) 75

Quiz 4: Answers

1. Clemson 2. Bank of America Stadium, Charlotte 3. Michigan Wolverines 4. UGA 34-10 Michigan 5. Miami 6. Alabama 7. Vanderbilt 8. Zamir White 9. James Cook 10. Brock Bowers 11. Robert Beal 12. Nakobe Dean and Travon Walker 13. Jordan Davis 14. Brock Bowers 15. Jordan Davis, Devonte Wyatt and Nakobe Dean 16. JT Daniels 17. Carson Beck 18. Derion Kendrick 19. c) 579 points 20. c) 5th

Quiz 6: Quarterbacks

1. Who is Georgia's all-time leader in passing yards?

2. In a 1993 game against Southern Miss, who became the first Georgia QB to throw for over 500 yards in a single game?

3. Who set a school record in 2004 after throwing 214 consecutive passes without an interception?

4. Aaron Murray is one of only two Bulldogs quarterback to throw 30 or more TD passes in a single season. Who is the other?

5. True or false – The Bulldogs have never passed for more than 4,000 yards in a single season?

6. Who was the starting quarterback on the 1980 National Championship-winning team?

7. Who is the only Bulldogs QB to throw for more than 3,000 yards in his freshman season?

8. Which Georgia quarterback was selected with the first overall pick of the 2009 NFL Draft?

9. Which Georgia quarterback went on to enjoy a stellar 18-year NFL career with the Vikings and Giants and was named the League MVP in 1975?

10. In 2011, Aaron Murray threw five touchdown passes in the first half of a game against which opponent?

11. What does the D in the name of quarterback D.J. Shockley stand for?

12. Which quarterback started the 2020 season opener but was later benched and subsequently transferred to Temple?

13. Which freshman quarterback led the 2017 Bulldogs to the National Championship Game?

14. Which quarterback set a school record in 2015 after completing 22 consecutive passes?

15. Stetson Bennett tied a school record after throwing five TD passes in the first half of a September 2021 game against which opponent?

16. Who was the last Bulldogs quarterback to receive All-American honors?

17. Which member of the Green Bay Packers Hall of Fame holds the Bulldogs record for throwing the most interceptions in a season with 29?

18. Who threw 5 TD passes and rushed for another in a 2005 game against Boise State?

19. Which of the following QBs threw the most career TD passes while a Bulldog? a) David Greene b) Matthew Stafford c) Eric Zeier

20. What is the highest number of TD passes thrown by Bulldogs quarterbacks in a single season? a) 37 b) 38 c) 39

Quiz 5: Answers

1. Stetson Bennett 2. Vince Dooley 3. 2010 4. Wallace Butts and Harry Mehre 5. White 6. 1940 7. Kentucky 8. Tyson Browning 9. David Greene 10. Jonathan Tyler 11. Steadman 12. 1988 13. True 14. Brock Bowers 15. Fran Tarkenton 16. Brock Bowers 17. True 18. 11 games 19. b) Bulldog Nation 20. b) 73

Quiz 7: Pot Luck

1. The field at Sanford Stadium is named after which former coach and athletic director?

2. The 2017 Bulldogs reached the National Championship Game after a wild 54-48 double overtime win over which opponent?

3. Who rushed for 1,385 yards and 17 touchdowns in his freshman season in 2012?

4. Who served as the interim head coach for the final game of the 2015 season, steering the Bulldogs to a win in the TaxSlayer Bowl?

5. In a 2009 game against Florida, the Bulldogs wore what color helmets for the first time?

6. Which UGA kicker went on to score 1,208 points in the NFL with the Bears and Cardinals?

7. Who returned an interception 99 yards for a touchdown in a 2003 game against Auburn?

8. True or False – Bulldogs special teams coordinator Scott Cochran had previously been a strength coach with the NBA's Charlotte Hornets?

9. Do the Bulldogs have an overall winning or losing record in road games?

10. Who succeeded Vince Dooley as the UGA head coach?

11. Which Georgia kicker holds the SEC record after converting 200 successive extra points?

12. True or false – Georgia alum Hines Ward made a cameo appearance in the 2012 'Batman' movie 'The Dark Knight Rises'?

13. Who is the elder of the two Stinchcomb brothers to have played for UGA in the late 1990s?

14. Up to the close of the 2021 season how many times had the Bulldogs won the SEC Championship?

15. Which Bulldog holds the NCAA record for the most rushing touchdowns by a freshman?

16. The longest TD run during the 2021 season was a 59-yard effort against Georgia Tech by which rusher?

17. Who was the only Bulldog to catch more than one touchdown pass in a single game during the 2021 season?

18. The Bulldogs set a home attendance record in a 2019 game against which opponent?

19. What was the first opponent to defeat the Bulldogs at Sanford Stadium? a) Alabama b) Georgia Tech c) Tulane

20. What is the most points Georgia has scored in a single game? a) 88 b) 98 c) 108

Quiz 6: Answers

1. Aaron Murray 2. Eric Zeier 3. David Greene 4. Jake Fromm 5. False 6. Buck Belue 7. Aaron Murray 8. Matthew Stafford 9. Fran Tarkenton 10. New Mexico State 11. Donald 12. D'Wan Mathis 13. Jake Fromm 14. Greyson Lambert 15. UAB Blazers 16. Eric Zeier 17. Zeke Bratkowski 18. D.J. Shockley 19. a) David Greene 20. c) 39 TDs

Quiz 8: Running Backs

1. Who is Georgia's all-time leading rusher?

2. Who holds the school record for scoring the most rushing touchdowns in a single season?

3. How many TDs did he score to set that record?

4. Herschel Walker rushed for a record 283 yards in a 1980 game against which SEC opponent?

5. Of backs with at least 200 carries, who has the best career yards per rush average?

6. Who holds the school record for the most career rushing touchdowns?

7. How many TDs did he score to set that record?

8. Which former Georgia back was named the NFL Offensive Rookie of the Year for 2015?

9. Who holds the record for the most rushing yards by a Bulldogs senior?

10. Who set a school record in 2010 after rushing for five TDs in a single game?

11. He set that single game scoring record in a game against which opponent?

12. Which pair of seniors both broke the 1,000-yard mark in the 2017 season?

13. True or false – In a 1974 game against South Carolina the Bulldogs rushed for over 500 yards?

14. Which Bulldog was selected by the Denver Broncos with the 12th overall pick of the 2009 NFL Draft?

15. Who was the last Bulldogs freshman to break the 1,000-yard barrier?

16. Which back's 89-yard run against Florida in 1985 is the longest TD run in school history?

17. Since 2000, who is the only Bulldog to lead the SEC in rushing?

18. Herschel Walker is one of only two Bulldogs to rush for over 1,000 yards in a season three times. Who is the other?

19. Which of the following backs had the most career rushing yards while a Bulldog? a) Todd Gurley b) Rodney Hampton c) Sony Michel

20. In a 1967 game against Kentucky, the Bulldogs set an SEC record after rushing how many times? a) 79 b) 89 c) 99

Quiz 7: Answers

1. Vince Dooley 2. Oklahoma 3. Todd Gurley 4. Bryan McClendon 5. Black 6. Kevin Butler 7. Odell Thurman 8. True 9. Winning 10. Ray Goff 11. Rodrigo Blankenship 12. True 13. Matt 14. 13 times 15. Herschel Walker 16. Kenny McIntosh 17. Brock Bowers 18. Notre Dame 19. c) Tulane 20. c) 108

Quiz 9: Pot Luck

1. What are the official colors of the Georgia Bulldogs?

2. Who are the three former Bulldogs to have won the Super Bowl MVP Award?

3. Which former walk-on kicker for the Bulldogs made his NFL debut with the Indianapolis Colts in 2020?

4. The #21 jersey has been retired in honor of which player?

5. The Bulldogs secured their 800th all-time win in September 2017, defeating which SEC rival by a score of 41-0?

6. Which Georgia running back represented the US in the 110-metres hurdles at the 2011 World Youth Athletics Championships?

7. Which opponent did the Bulldogs defeat in the 'Hobnail Boot Game'?

8. Who caught the TD pass to give the Bulldogs the win in that famous game?

9. Who threw that game-winning TD pass?

10. What color pants did the Bulldogs wear in the 2021/22 National Championship Game?

11. Who is the only Bulldog to have scored multiple rushing touchdowns of 81 yards or more?

12. Do the Bulldogs have a winning or losing record in games played at neutral venues?

13. Who was the first head coach to steer the Bulldogs to four straight Bowl Game wins?

14. Of UGA head coaches with at least 50 victories, who has the best win percentage?

15. Which UGA Pro Football Hall of Famer was also Georgia's baseball coach in the late 1940s?

16. Which member of the College Hall of Fame had spells as head coach of East Carolina, Wyoming and most famously, Auburn, and was an All-American, two-way starter with the Bulldogs in the 1950s?

17. In what decade did the Bulldogs win their first Bowl Game?

18. True or false – During the 2021 season, the Bulldogs smashed non-conference opponents by a combined score of 157-14?

19. In what year did the Bulldogs play their first ever game? a) 1892 b) 1893 c) 1894

20. Which opponent did Georgia face in that historic encounter? a) Alabama b) Mercer c) Vanderbilt

Quiz 8: Answers

1. Herschel Walker 2. Garrison Hearst 3. 19 TDs 4. Vanderbilt 5. D'Andre Swift 6. Herschel Walker 7. 49 TDs 8. Todd Gurley 9. Nick Chubb 10. Washaun Ealey 11. Kentucky 12. Nick Chubb and Sony Michel 13. True 14. Knowshon Moreno 15. Nick Chubb 16. Tim Worley 17. Knowshon Moreno 18. Nick Chubb 19. c) Sony Michel 20. b) 89 times

Quiz 10: Receivers

1. Who is Georgia's all-time leader in receiving yards with 3,093?

2. Whose 76 catches in 1993 are the most in a single season by a Bulldogs receiver?

3. Who tied a school record in a 2008 game against Georgia Tech after catching a hat-trick of touchdowns?

4. Which receiver's 56 catches in 2008 are the most by a Bulldogs freshman?

5. In a 2001 game against Kentucky who became the first UGA receiver with 200 receiving yards in a single game?

6. Who beat that record after bagging 205 yards in a 2015 game against Michigan State?

7. Who was the first Bulldog to catch more than 10 touchdowns in a single season?

8. Who caught an 80-yard touchdown pass in the College Football Championship Game in January 2018?

9. Whose 15 catches in a 1993 game against Florida are the most by a Bulldog in a single game?

10. Who was the last Georgia wide receiver to be selected in the first round of the NFL Draft?

11. Who tied a school record after catching 12 passes in the 2020 Sugar Bowl against Baylor?

12. The longest reception in school history was a 98-yard TD against North Texas in 2013 which was caught by which receiver?

13. Which quarterback threw that record long pass?

14. Before Brock Bowers in 2021, who was the last Bulldog with 800 receiving yards in a single season?

15. True or false – Georgia receiver Ladd McConkey is the son of long-time New York Giants receiver Phil McConkey?

16. Whose 87-yard touchdown catch against Nebraska in the 2013 Capital One Bowl is the longest by a Bulldog in a Bowl Game?

17. Which Georgia tight end was selected in the first round of the 2004 NFL Draft and went on to have a stellar 15-year career?

18. Who is the only Bulldogs receiver with more than 200 career receptions?

19. Which of the following receivers had the most catches while with the Bulldogs? a) Reggie Brown b) Fred Gibson c) Malcolm Mitchell

20. Former Bulldogs receiver Hines Ward was born in which Asian capital? a) Manila b) Seoul c) Tokyo

Quiz 9: Answers

1. Red and Black 2. Jake Scott, Terrell Davis and Hines Ward 3. Rodrigo Blankenship 4. Frank Sinkwich 5. Tennessee 6. Todd Gurley 7. Tennessee 8. Verron Haynes 9. David Greene 10. Silver 11. Nick Chubb 12. Winning 13. Jim Donnan 14. Kirby Smart 15. Charley Trippi 16. Pat Dye 17. 1940s 18. True 19. a) 1892 20. b) Mercer

Quiz 11: Pot Luck

1. What is the name of the team's canine mascot?

2. The #62 jersey has been retired in honor of which legendary Bulldog?

3. In what decade did the Bulldogs first appear in a televised game?

4. What do the letters A.J. stand for in the name of Bulldogs receiver A.J. Green?

5. Which Bulldog holds the SEC record for throwing the most career touchdown passes?

6. Which Bulldogs quarterback from the mid-1990s went on to become Georgia's offensive coordinator from 2007 to 2014?

7. What color are the numbers on Georgia's white jersey?

8. In what decade was the SEC founded?

9. True or false – Georgia was a founder member of the SEC?

10. The Bulldogs set a school record across the 1997 and 1998 seasons after winning how many consecutive road games?

11. Which Bulldog finished in fifth place on the ballot for the 1983 Heisman Trophy, at that time the highest ever position for a defensive back?

12. Which All-American offensive guard from the mid-1970s shares a name with a pitcher who spent 22 seasons in the Majors from 1988 to 2009?

13. Before he become head coach in Georgia Jim Donnan had won a Division I-AA National Championship with which program?

14. The Bulldogs were last involved in a tied game in November 1994. Against which opponent did UGA share a 23-23 scoreline?

15. Which head coach guided UGA to 140 victories between 1939 and 1960?

16. After leaving Georgia Herschel Walker began his pro career with which USFL team?

17. 2021 National Championship defensive back Derion Kendrick transferred to Georgia from which school?

18. What was the fewest points that the Bulldogs scored in a single game during the 2021 season?

19. In what year was the University of Georgia founded? a) 1785 b) 1795 b) 1805

20. In 2021, the Bulldogs set a record after how many of their players were selected in the NFL Draft? a) seven b) eight c) nine

Quiz 10: Answers

1. Terrence Edwards 2. Brice Hunter 3. Mohamed Massaquoi 4. A.J. Green 5. Fred Gibson 6. Tavarres King 7. Terrence Edwards 8. Mecole Hardman 9. Shannon Mitchell 10. A.J. Green 11. George Pickens 12. Reggie Davis 13. David Greene 14. Malcolm Mitchell 15. False 16. Chris Conley 17. Benjamin Watson 18. Terrence Edwards 19. c) Malcolm Mitchell 20. b) Seoul

Quiz 12: Defense

1.Whose 14.5 sacks in 2012 are the most in a single season by a Georgia defender?

2. Which defensive back started 53 games between 2014 and 2017, the most in the history of Georgia football?

3. Which All-American set a school record in 1982 after picking off 12 passes?

4. Who is the only Bulldogs defender to have received All-American honors three times?

5. How many shutouts did the Bulldogs register during the 2021 National Championship-winning season?

6. True or false – In a 1943 game against Presbyterian the Bulldogs set an SEC record after picking off nine passes?

7. Which award-winning linebacker registered his first pick six in an October 2021 game against Florida?

8. Who holds the school record for the most sacks in a single game after registering five in a 1983 contest against Temple?

9. What was the given name of Bulldogs linebacker Boss Bailey?

10. True or false – In a 1999 game against Kentucky the Bulldogs defense held the opposition to minus 50 rushing yards?

11. Which DB scored two interception return touchdowns during the 2020 season?

12. Which DB famously returned a fumble 92 yards for a score in a 2003 game against Tennessee?

13. Which former Bulldogs defensive lineman, who was drafted by the Patriots with the sixth pick of the 2001 NFL Draft, finished in 131st place in the 2019 World Series of Poker Main Event?

14. Which versatile defender / receiver and future NFL superstar played over 1,000 snaps for the Bulldogs during the 1998 season?

15. Which dominant defender was named the SEC Defensive Player of the Year in both 2002 and 2004?

16. Which linebacker set a school record after registering 26 tackles in a 1983 game against Georgia Tech?

17. Up to the close of the 2021 season, who was the last Bulldog with double digit sacks in a single season?

18. Who is Georgia's all-time leader in tackles after recording 467 between 1974 and 1977?

19. What is the highest number of interceptions the Bulldogs have registered in a single season? a) 33 b) 34 c) 35

20. What is the highest number of sacks the Bulldogs have registered in a single season? a) 51 b) 52 c) 53

Quiz 11: Answers

1. Uga 2. Charley Trippi 3. 1950s 4. Adriel Jeremiah 5. Aaron Murray 6. Mike Bobo 7. Black 8. 1930s 9. True 10. Eight 11. Terry Hoage 12. Randy Johnson 13. Marshall 14. Auburn 15. Wallace Butts 16. New Jersey Generals 17. Clemson 18. 10 points 19. a) 1785 20. c) Nine

Quiz 13: Pot Luck

1. True or false – Up to and including 2022, the Bulldogs had the longest active streak of appearing in a Bowl Game?

2. The main campus of the University of Georgia is situated in a town that shares its name with the capital city of which country?

3. What number jersey did legendary running back Herschel Walker wear?

4. Do the Bulldogs have an overall winning or losing record in games played on artificial turf?

5. Which defender leapt almost 4ft in the air to famously block a field goal in an October 2002 game against Tennessee?

6. True or false – Star 1990s running back Robert Edwards began his college career as a defensive back?

7. What color is the facemask on the Bulldogs helmet?

8. The game between Georgia and which opponent was unofficially known as 'The World's Largest Outdoor Cocktail Party'?

9. True or false – Sanford Stadium has the largest capacity in the SEC?

10. Between 1980 and 1983 the Bulldogs won how many SEC games in a row?

11. Which Bulldogs special teamer won Academic All-American honors in 2019?

12. What does the J in the name of former Georgia defensive back J.R. Reed stand for?

13. Who is the only UGA head coach to have won the Walter Camp Coach of the Year Award?

14. Stetson Bennett scored his only rushing touchdown during the 2021 season against which SEC opponent?

15. Pass rusher Jarvis Jones arrived at Georgia as a sophomore after spending his freshman season with which school?

16. Nolan Smith against Missouri in 2021 was the last Bulldog to do what?

17. Which linebacker registered a hat-trick of sacks in the 2021 win over Tennessee?

18. In 2004, which Bulldog defender became the inaugural winner of the Lott IMPACT Award?

19. What is the name of the bell that is traditionally rung following a Bulldogs victory? a) Chapel Bell b) Church Bell c) College Bell

20. What is the capacity of Sanford Stadium? a) 90,746 b) 91,746 c) 92,746

Quiz 12: Answers

1. Jarvis Jones 2. Dominick Sanders 3. Terry Hoage 4. David Pollack 5. Three 6. True 7. Nakobe Dean 8. Freddie Gilbert 9. Rodney 10. True 11. Eric Stokes 12. Sean Jones 13. Richard Seymour 14. Champ Bailey 15. David Pollack 16. Knox Culpepper 17. Jarvis Jones 18. Ben Zambiasi 19. c) 35 interceptions 20. b) 52

Quiz 14: Special Teams

1. Who was the kicker on the 2021 and 2022 National Championship teams?

2. In 2009, who became the first Bulldog in school history to return a kickoff 100 yards for a touchdown?

3. Which defensive star blocked a school record four field goals between 1980 and 1983?

4. Whose 440 career points are the most by a Bulldogs kicker?

5. Which Bulldog was the first kicker inducted into the College Football Hall of Fame?

6. Which star running back returned kickoffs for 100-yard touchdowns against Buffalo in 2012 and Clemson in 2014?

7. Prior to the start of the 2022 season, who was the last Bulldog to return a kickoff for a touchdown?

8. And who was the last Bulldog to return a punt for a touchdown?

9. Which former Bulldogs placekicker appeared in 301 games during an NFL career that lasted some 20 seasons?

10. Who holds the school record for the most career kickoff return touchdowns?

11. Which defensive back tied a school record in 2003 after blocking three punts?

12. Which fellow defender, and member of a famous footballing family, had managed the same feat during the previous season?

13. Which Georgia kicker converted an SEC record 215 PATs between 2012 and 2015?

14. Who boomed punts for a Bulldogs best 48.1-yard average during the 2009 season?

15. Who holds the record for the most successful field goals in a single game after converting six against Georgia Tech in 2001?

16. Whose 227 punts between 2003 and 2006 are the most in school history?

17. Which Georgia kicker converted a field goal in 45 games between 2008 and 2011, the most in the history of NCAA football?

18. Who was the punter on the 2021 National Championship team?

19. What is the longest successful field goal in school history? a) 59 yards b) 60 yards c) 61 yards

20. Which kicker converted that record-breaking field goal? a) Billy Bennett b) Rodrigo Blankenship c) Kevin Butler

Quiz 13: Answers

1. True 2. Greece 3. #34 4. Winning 5. Boss Bailey 6. True 7. White 8. Florida 9. False 10. 23 games 11. Rodrigo Blankenship 12. Jake 13. Vince Dooley 14. Tennessee 15. USC 16. Score a safety 17. Channing Tindall 18. David Pollack 19. a) Chapel Bell 20. c) 92,746

Quiz 15: Pot Luck

1. Who is the play-by-play announcer on Georgia Bulldogs radio broadcasts?

2. Which former QB is the color analyst on the Georgia Bulldogs radio network?

3. 'The Drought Breaker' was the nickname of which legendary Bulldog who played for the team in the late 1950s?

4. In 2017, who became the first Bulldog to win the Butkus Award which is given to the nation's top linebacker?

5. Which linebacker and future NFL star returned a fumble 96 yards for a touchdown in an October 2015 game against Tennessee?

6. Do the Bulldogs have a winning or losing record in games that have gone to overtime?

7. Which Bulldog set an NCAA record in 2003 after converting 31 field goals?

8. What do the three arms of the famous Georgia Arch represent?

9. True or false – Actor Samuel L. Jackson is a big fan of the Bulldogs?

10. What is the name of Georgia's costumed mascot?

11. In what decade did this costumed mascot appear for the first time?

12. The Okefenokee Oar is awarded to the winner of games between Georgia and which opponent?

13. Which Bulldog was named the SEC Special Teams Player of the Year 2020?

14. True or false – Former Bulldogs running back Nick Chubb is the brother of Miami Dolphins pass rusher Bradley Chubb?

15. Which Bulldog is the only multiple winner of the Ted Hendricks Award, which is given to college football's top edge rusher?

16. Which linebacker returned a blocked field goal for a 55-yard touchdown in a 2012 game against Alabama?

17. How many minutes before home games does 'The Lone Trumpeter' play the opening notes of 'Battle Hymn of the Republic'?

18. Who holds the Bulldogs record for the most successful field goals of 50 yards or more?

19. How much did Sanford Stadium originally cost to build? a) $36,000 b) $360,000 c) $3.6 million

20. What was the name of Georgia's first head coach? a) Charles Herty b) Henry Herty c) William Herty

Quiz 14: Answers

1. Jack Podlesny 2. Brandon Boykin 3. Terry Hoage 4. Rodrigo Blankenship 5. Kevin Butler 6. Todd Gurley 7. Isaiah McKenzie 8. Mecole Hardman 9. John Casey 10. Brandon Boykin 11. Sean Jones 12. Boss Bailey 13. Marshall Morgan 14. Drew Butler 15. Billy Bennett 16. Gordon Ely-Kelso 17. Blair Walsh 18. Jake Camarda 19. b) 60 yards 20. c) Kevin Butler

Quiz 16: Bulldogs in the NFL

1. Which former Bulldog is the only player in NFL history with 2,000 rushing yards and 20 TDs in a single season?

2. Herschel Walker had spells with which four NFL teams?

3. Which defensive lineman won three Super Bowls with the Patriots before being traded to the Raiders in 2009?

4. In 1943, who became the first Bulldog to be selected with the first overall pick of the NFL Draft?

5. Who is the only Bulldogs quarterback to go on to appear in three Super Bowls?

6. Which former Bulldog finished behind only Derrick Henry after rushing for 1,494 yards during the 2019 season?

7. Which Bulldogs alum is second in the Cincinnati Bengals record book for receiving yards, receiving touchdowns, and receptions?

8. Which linebacker, who spent four seasons with the Chicago Bears, enjoyed his first double-digit sack season in 2021 with the Los Angeles Rams?

9. In 2011, which former Bulldog became just the fifth quarterback in NFL history to pass for over 5,000 yards in a single season?

10. Which durable former Georgia full back played in 201 games between 1993 and 2007 for the Seattle Seahawks?

11. Which linebacker won a Super Bowl with the 2013 Ravens then another one with the 2018 Eagles?

12. Which Bulldogs defensive star was elected to 12 Pro Bowls between 2001 and 2013 during a stellar NFL career?

13. Which offensive tackle did the New York Giants select with the fourth overall pick of the 2020 NFL Draft?

14. Who was the last Georgia running back to be picked in the first round of the NFL Draft?

15. Who was last Bulldogs kicker to be selected in the NFL Draft? (clue: it was in 2012?

16. If all the former Georgia players to appear in the NFL were listed alphabetically which offensive star would be last on the list?

17. Which former Bulldog is the all-time leader in receptions for the Pittsburgh Steelers?

18. Which undrafted Georgia offensive lineman won a pair of Super Bowl rings with the Patriots in the late 1990s?

19. Which former Bulldog was the winner of the 2014 Walter Payton NFL Man of the Year Award? a) Thomas Davis b) Richard Seymour c) Matthew Stafford

20. Up to and including the 2021 Draft, which NFL team had selected the fewest number of players from UGA? a) Broncos b) Chargers c) Raiders

Quiz 15: Answers

1. Scott Howard 2. Eric Zeier 3. Theron Sapp 4. Roquan Smith 5. Leonard Floyd 6. Winning 7. Billy Bennett 8. Wisdom, Justice and Moderation 9. True 10. Hairy Dawg 11. 1980s 12. Florida 13. Jake Camarda 14. False – They're cousins 15. David Pollack 16. Alec Ogletree 17. Seven minutes 18. Kevin Butler 19. b) $360,000 20. a) Charles Herty

Quiz 17: Pot Luck

1. Before becoming head coach at Georgia, Kirby Smart had been the defensive coordinator at which college?

2. Which opponent have the Bulldogs faced the most times in school history?

3. Who is the only Bulldog to have won the Bronko Nagurski Award which is given by the Football Writers Association of America to the top defensive player in college football? (Clue: It was in 1998)

4. Which running back's 248 carries for 1,334 yards and 14 TDs plus 20 catches for another 253 yards were enough to give him the SEC Freshman of the Year award in 2007?

5. Who holds the school record for the most career punt return touchdowns with five?

6. What color helmet did the Bulldogs wear in the 2011 season opener against Boise State?

7. The Bulldogs wore what unusual color pants in that game?

8. Games between Georgia and Georgia Tech are traditionally played on the weekend closes to which holiday?

9. Who returned a fumble 99 yards for a touchdown in a 2014 game against Georgia Tech?

10. Since it opened have the Bulldogs lost fewer or more than 100 games at Sanford Stadium?

11. Herschel Walker holds the NCAA record for the most 200-yard + games by a freshman. How many times did he break the 200-yard barrier in 1980?

12. Which former Bulldog is one of just four quarterbacks in NFL history to have thrown five TD passes in a game in his rookie season?

13. Which former Georgia linebacker delivered the hit that injured Drew Bledsoe and heralded the start of the Tom Brady era in New England?

14. Stetson Bennett topped 300 yards passing against two opponents during the 2021 season. Which two?

15. Which Bulldogs cornerback gave up just a single touchdown catch on over 1,000 coverage snaps between 2015 and 2018?

16. Which former Bulldog was named the 1944 NFL MVP?

17. Which receiver threw and caught a touchdown pass in a 2016 game against Penn State?

18. The #40 jersey has been retired in honor of which legendary full back?

19. What type of privet is present at Sanford Stadium? a) Chinese Privet b) Indian Privet c) Japanese Privet

20. In 2017, the Bulldogs set a school record after rushing for how many yards? a) 3,676 b) 3,776 c) 3,876

Quiz 16: Answers

1. Terrell Davis 2. Cowboys, Vikings, Eagles and Giants 3. Richard Seymour 4. Frank Sinkwich 5. Fran Tarkenton 6. Nick Chubb 7. A.J. Green 8. Leonard Floyd 9. Matthew Stafford 10. Mack Strong 11. Dannell Ellerbe 12. Champ Bailey 13. Andrew Thomas 14. Sony Michel 15. Blair Walsh 16. Eric Zeier 17. Hines Ward 18. David Andrews 19. a) Thomas Davis 20. c) Raiders

Quiz 18: Circle of Honor

1. Which legendary coach was also the UGA's Director of Athletics from 1979 to 2004?

2. Which freshman DB and future NFL star blocked a field goal in the game that sealed the 1980 National Championship?

3. In 1913, which halfback became the first Georgia football player to receive All-American recognition?

4. Which former Bulldogs quarterback was the coach of the Oakland Raiders team that reached Super Bowl II?

5. Which quarterback and future NFL star threw 18 TD passes and rushed for 10 more during his career at UGA from 1958 to 1960?

6. Which All-American halfback continued to play during the 1941 season despite suffering a broken jaw?

7. In 1968, which future Super Bowl winner with Miami became the first Bulldog to win the Outland Trophy which is awarded to college football's top interior lineman?

8. Which member of the Circle of Honor returned to campus in 2018 to complete a degree in economics, 34 years after he left the Bulldogs to start his NFL career?

9. Which four-sport letterman and All-American End from the 1950s shares a name with a legendary talk show host?

10. 'Catfish' was the nickname of which former Bulldogs football star who later went on to coach the school's baseball and basketball teams?

11. Which two-time All American defensive tackle from the 1960s has the same name as a noted US WWII General?

12. Which Bulldog was the backup QB on the Green Bay Packers teams that won Super Bowls I and II?

13. The award given to UGA athletes who distinguished themselves as alumni is named after which versatile player from the 1930s who later became the Bulldogs kicking coach?

14. In 1994, who became just the third quarterback in NCAA Division I to throw for more than 11,000 yards in his career?

15. Who are the only pair of brothers in the Circle of Honor?

16. The career of which versatile Bulldog from the 1990s included 203 rushes, 144 catches, 71 passes and 48 kick returns?

17. Which Bulldog won a Purple Heart, Bronze Star & the Distinguished Service Cross for his actions in the Battle of the Bulge in WW2?

18. Which tailback and returner from the 1950s was also the first Georgia basketball player to receive All-American honors?

19. Which Bulldogs linebacker would later go on to win Canada's Grey Cup and become a member of the Canadian Football Hall of Fame?

20. Which defensive end later became the head of the Atlanta Committee for the Olympic Games and the chairman of Augusta National Gold Club?

Quiz 17: Answers

1. Alabama 2. Auburn 3. Champ Bailey 4. Knowshon Moreno 5. Isaiah McKenzie 6. Silver 7. Red 8. Thanksgiving 9. Damian Swann 10. More than 100 11. Four times 12. Matthew Stafford 13. Mo Lewis 14. Alabama and Michigan 15. Deandre Baker 16. Frank Sinkwich 17. Terry Godwin 18. Theron Sapp 19. a) Chinese Privet 20. c) 3,876

Quiz 19: Pot Luck

1. Kirby Smart spent a season as an assistant head coach at which NFL team?

2. Only one team has appeared in more Bowl Games than the Bulldogs. Which one?

3. Which opponent has UGA defeated the most times in school history?

4. Which three Bulldogs were selected in the first round of the 2018 NFL Draft?

5. Which former Georgia defender was elected to the Pro Football Hall of Fame in the class of 2022?

6. Which dominant Georgia linebacker from 2007 to 2009 is the author of a book called 'Free Agent - The Perspectives of A Young African American Athlete'?

7. What was unusual about the jerseys worn by the Bulldogs in the 2011 season-opener against Boise State?

8. Which long-standing rival was the first opponent to beat the Bulldogs in a competitive game?

9. The Bulldogs suffered a record 0-60 defeat in a 1931 game at which west coast opponent?

10. True or false – Sanford Stadium hosted games at soccer's 1994 FIFA World Cup?

11. Which head coach has guided the Bulldogs to the most career wins?

12. Who is second on that last of most career wins?

13. What was quarterback Buck Belue's given first name?

14. Which Georgia DB went on to have a stellar NFL career with Miami and Washington in the 1970s, including 35 picks and two Super Bowl rings?

15. Which UGA all-time great celebrated his 100th birthday in December 2021?

16. Stetson Bennett threw his first touchdown pass as a Bulldog to which receiver?

17. True or false – The Bulldogs didn't give up a single penalty in the 2021 game against Georgia Tech?

18. Who intercepted three passes in a 2006 game against Auburn?

19. Who holds the record for the most points by a Bulldogs kicker in a single season? a) Kevin Butler b) Billy Bennett c) Jack Podlesny

20. How many points did he score to set that record? a) 131 b) 141 c) 151

Quiz 18: Answers

1. Vince Dooley 2. Terry Hoage 3. Bob McWhorter 4. John Rauch 5. Fran Tarkenton 6. Frank Sinkwich 7. Bill Stanfill 8. Kevin Butler 9. Johnny Carson 10. Vernon Smith 11. George Patton 12. Zeke Bratkowski 13. Bill Hartman 14. Eric Zeier 15. Matt and Jon Stinchcomb 16. Hines Ward 17. George Poschner 18. Zippy Morocco 19. Ben Zambiasi 20. Billy Payne

Quiz 20: 1980 National Champions

1. The Bulldogs secured the 1980 National Championship with a Sugar Bowl win over which opponent?

2. What was the game's final score?

3. Who was named the game's MVP?

4. The Sugar Bowl finale was played at which famous venue?

5. Who was the head coach of the 1980 National Championship team?

6. Who was the quarterback in 11 of the 12 games during the 1980 season?

7. One other quarterback threw a touchdown pass that year. Which one?

8. The Bulldogs secured the 1980 SEC title with a 31-21 road win over which opponent?

9. Who was the kicker on the 1980 National Championship team?

10. True or False – Coca Cola released a special bottle to honor Georgia's 1980 National Championship win?

11. Which defensive star returned a punt 67 yards for a touchdown and returned an interception 98 yards (but didn't score) against Clemson that year?

12. Who led the National Champions with eight interceptions in 1980?

13. Who led the team in touchdown receptions in 1980 with four?

14. The Bulldogs opened the season with the 16-15 road win at which SEC rival?

15. True or false – No team scored more than 21 points against the Bulldogs throughout the whole of the 1980 season?

16. On what day of the week did the Sugar Bowl take place?

17. In their preseason poll, AP had the Bulldogs ranked at what position?

18. True or false – Herschel Walker scored more touchdowns than the rest of the Bulldogs team combined?

19. How many passes did the Bulldogs complete in the Sugar Bowl? a) zero b) one c) two

20. How many total passing yards did the Bulldogs amass in the Sugar Bowl? a) 7 b) 17 c) 27

Quiz 19: Answers

1. Miami Dolphins 2. Alabama 3. Georgia Tech 4. Roquan Smith, Isaiah Wynn and Sony Michel 5. Richard Seymour 6. Rennie Curran 7. Instead of the player's name, each jersey featured the word Georgia 8. Auburn 9. USC 10. False 11. Vince Dooley 12. Mark Richt 13. Benjamin 14. Jake Scott 15. Charley Trippi 16. Demetris Robinson 17. True 18. Tra Battle 19. c) Jack Podlesny 20. c) 151 points

Quiz 21: Pot Luck

1. Who was the first Bulldogs head coach to lead the team to three straight seasons with 11 or more wins?

2. Which Bulldogs defensive back and member of the Pro Football Hall of Fame was elected to the College Football Hall of Fame as part of the class of 2022?

3. The Bulldogs have suffered more defeats against which opponent than any other?

4. Who was the only Bulldog selected in the first round of the 2021 NFL Draft? (clue: He was picked by the Packers)

5. The award given to the Georgia Bulldogs MVP is named after which former coach?

6. Which Bulldogs receiver, who caught 158 passes for 2,282 yards between 2005 and 2008, later had to have four fingers amputated after an auto accident?

7. Which Bulldog is the co-holder of the SEC record for the most kickoff return touchdowns in a single season with three?

8. In what decade did the current oval G logo first appear on the Bulldogs helmet?

9. True or false – The Bulldogs have never worn black pants as part of their gameday uniform?

10. In what decade did Georgia face Georgia Tech for the first time?

11. Who won that historic encounter?

12. Who was the last Bulldogs head coach with an overall losing record?

13. Who is the only Bulldog to have won the Walter Camp Award which is given by NCAA coaches to the top player in college football?

14. In 2002, who famously batted down a pass from South Carolina quarterback Corey Jenkins in the end zone then grabbed the pass to score a touchdown?

15. Which versatile former Bulldog was the winner of the 2011 season of the TV talent show, 'Dancing With The Stars'?

16. Which former UGA great was the author of an autobiography called 'No Time for Losing' and a mystery novel 'Murder at the Super Bowl'?

17. Stetson Bennett scored his first rushing touchdown as a Bulldog in a 63-17 win over which FCS school in September 2019?

18. The stingy Georgia defense gave up just 2 rushing yards in a 2021 game against which #3 ranked opponent?

19. What breed is the Bulldogs' famous mascot? a) English Bulldog b) French Bulldog c) Valley Bulldog

20. How long is the longest punt in Bulldogs history? a) 67 yards b) 77 yards c) 87 yards

Quiz 20: Answers

1. Notre Dame 2. Bulldogs 17-10 Fighting Irish 3. Herschel Walker 4. Louisiana Superdome 5. Vince Dooley 6. Buck Belue 7. Jeff Paulk 8. Auburn 9. Rex Robinson 10. True 11. Scott Woerner 12. Jeff Hipp 13. Amp Arnold 14. Tennessee 15. True 16. Thursday 17. 16th 18. False 19. b) One 20. a) 7 yards

Quiz 22: Numbers Game

What number jersey did the following Georgia greats wear?

1. Hines Ward

2. Eric Zeier

3. Terrell Davis

4. Terrence Edwards

5. Aaron Murray

6. Todd Gurley

7. Champ Bailey

8. Richard Seymour

9. Matthew Stafford

10. David Pollack

11. Charley Trippi

12. Justin Houston

13. Sony Michel

14. Terry Hoage

15. Jake Scott

16. A.J. Green

17. Garrison Hearst

18. Roquan Smith

19. Nick Chubb

20. Lindsay Scott

Quiz 21: Answers

1. Kirby Smart 2. Champ Bailey 3. Auburn 4. Eric Stokes 5. Vince Dooley
6. Mohamed Massaquoi. 7. Brandon Boykin 8. 1960s 9. False 10. 1890s
11. Georgia Tech 12. Johnny Griffith 13. Herschel Walker 14. David
Pollack 15. Hines Ward 16. Fran Tarkenton 17. Murray State 18.
Clemson 19. a) English Bulldog 20. c) 87 yards

Quiz 23: Pot Luck

1. Between 2007 and 2010 Bulldogs offensive coordinator Todd Monken was the receivers coach at which NFL team?

2. Which Bulldog was the winner of the 1982 Heisman Trophy?

3. Who is the only former Bulldog to have later gone on to be named the NFL MVP?

4. The award given to the Bulldog who 'shows courage to overcome adversity' is named after which former defensive lineman who suffered a stroke during a 2001 practice?

5. Which freshman running back rushed for 100 yards or more in each of the final eight games of the 2014 season?

6. Who holds the school record for the most career return touchdowns (kickoffs and punts)?

7. Which punter, who later spent eight seasons in the NFL with the Oilers, Bills and Eagles, set the record for the longest punt in school history in a 1967 game against Auburn?

8. Between 1964 and 1979 the Georgia uniform featured what color pants?

9. The game known as 'The Deep South's Oldest Rivalry' is played between Georgia and which opponent?

10. True or false – Head coach Kirby Smart was a four-year letterman with the Bulldogs as a player?

11. Georgia's longest winning streak stretches to how many games?

12. True or False – The mascot for Georgia's first ever game was a goat?

13. After leaving Georgia Mark Richt went on to become the head coach of which team?

14. Which UGA quarterback was drafted by baseball's Chicago White Sox and later spent three seasons with the Montreal Expos organization?

15. Star pass rusher David Pollack was picked in the first round of the 2005 NFL Draft by which team?

16. True or false – Prior to the National Championship Game triumph, head coach Kirby Smart had an 0-4 record against opposite number Nick Saban?

17. In which round of the NFL Draft was Herschel Walker selected?

18. Who were the two quarterbacks to start for the Bulldogs during the 2021 season?

19. What was the first Bowl Game won by the Bulldogs? a) Orange Bowl b) Rose Bowl c) Sugar Bowl

20. Which opponent did the Bulldogs defeat to claim that maiden Bowl Game title? a) Texas A & M b) Texas Christian c) Texas Tech

Quiz 22: Answers

1. #19 2. #10 3. #33 4. #8 5. #11 6. #3 7. #4 8. #93 9. #7 10. #47 11. #62 12. #42 13. #1 14. #14 15. #13 16. #8 17. #5 18. #3 19. #27 20. #24

Quiz 24: Anagrams

Rearrange the letters to make the name of a Bulldogs great.

1. HER WHALE CLERKS

2. WRECKS OR BOB

3. WIN SHARED

4. VALID PADLOCK

5. A NAKED BONE

6. ECO STRIKES

7. DOCILE ENVOY

8. GRENADE DIVE

9. DWARF HAFTS TOTEM

10. ONLY CHIMES

11. TRULY DODGE

12. CENTERS REWARDED

13. TRY RIB MASK

14. BULKIER VENT

15. PALACE BY HIM

16. GEAR THEORY

17. HOIST ARRANGERS

18. AVOIDS MATHS

19. A BORED LOPING SHRINK

20. MERCURY HAIRDOS

Quiz 23: Answers

1. Jacksonville Jaguars 2. Herschel Walker 3. Terrell Davis 4. David Jacobs 5. Nick Chubb 6. Isaiah McKenzie 7. Spike Jones 8. White 9. Auburn 10. True 11. 17 games 12. True 13. Miami Hurricanes 14. Buck Belue 15. Cincinnati 16. True 17. Fifth 18. Stetson Bennett and J.T. Daniels 19. a) Orange Bowl 20. b) Texas Christian

Quiz 25: Pot Luck

1. Who was the defensive coordinator on the 2021 National Championship team?

2. Georgia's Indoor Athletic Facility is named after which notable Bulldogs family?

3. What is the most rushing touchdowns the Bulldogs have scored in a single game?

4. Which quarterback set an NCAA record in 2015 after completing 24 of 25 passes in a game against USC?

5. Which former Bulldogs linebacker was named the 2002 NFL Rookie of the Year?

6. Which future NFL star had 413 yards passing and 56 yards rushing in the 1995 Peach Bowl against Virginia?

7. True or false – Bulldogs defensive stars Boss and Champ Bailey are brothers?

8. Which running back blocked a punt in a September 2020 win over Arkansas?

9. The first overtime game in the history of the SEC took place in 1996 and featured Georgia and which opponent?

10. Georgia set a school record between 1980 and 1983 after winning how many straight home games?

11. Which linebacker scored a 96-yard fumble return touchdown in a 2015 game at Tennessee?

12. Do the Bulldogs have an all-time winning or losing record in games against Alabama?

13. Who had a 40-19 overall record as UGA's head coach between 1996 and 2000?

14. Who was the last Bulldogs head coach to have been born in the state of Georgia?

15. Which Bulldogs great heads a food company called 'Renaissance Man Food Services'?

16. 'The Mailman' is the nickname of which member of the 2021 National Championship team?

17. Who returned an interception 74 yards for a touchdown in the 2021 season opener?

18. Kirby Smart started his coaching career as an assistant at which NCAA Division II school in the Gulf South Conference?

19. What was the over/under in the 2021/22 National Title Decider? a) 50 points b) 52 points c) 54 points

20. What was head coach Kirby Smart's salary in 2021? a) $5.13 million b) $6.13 million c) $7.13 million

Quiz 24: Answers

1. Herschel Walker 2. Brock Bowers 3. Hines Ward 4. David Pollack 5. Nakobe Dean 6. Eric Stokes 7. Vince Dooley 8. David Greene 9. Matthew Stafford 10. Sony Michel 11. Todd Gurley 12. Terrence Edwards 13. Kirby Smart 14. Kevin Butler 15. Champ Bailey 16. Terry Hoage 17. Garrison Hearst 18. Thomas Davis 19. Rodrigo Blankenship 20. Richard Seymour

Bonus Questions

Bonus Quiz 1: 2023 National Championship Game

1. The Bulldogs secured a second straight national title after defeating which opponent in the 2023 College Football Playoff National Championship?

2. What was the final score in this one-sided encounter?

3. The National Championship was hosted at which stadium?

4. Who was named the game's offensive MVP?

5. Who was the game's defensive MVP?

6. Which pair of Bulldogs both scored two rushing touchdowns?

7. Who was the only offensive starter for the Bulldogs whose first name and surname start with the same letter?

8. Which Bulldog caught two touchdown passes in the National Championship Game?

9. Whose only catch resulted in a 22-yard touchdown with less than 30 seconds remaining in the first half?

10. True or false – The Bulldogs rushed for 252 yards in the National Championship Game but the leading individual back rushed for a total of 50 yards?

11. Which Bulldog picked off two passes in the big game?

12. With 11 catches for 152 yards and a touchdown, who was Georgia's leading pass catcher in the National Championship Game?

13. How many sacks did the Georgia defense register in the National Championship Game?

14. How many points did the Bulldogs score in the first half?

15. What was the last college prior to Georgia to repeat as National Champions?

16. Stetson Bennett tied which current NFL superstar's record of six combined passing and rushing touchdowns in a National Championship Game?

17. True or false – The Bulldogs set the record for the largest point differential win in the history of the National Championship Game?

18. Which a capella group performed 'The Star-Spangled Banner' at the National Championship?

19. The Bulldogs restricted TCU to how many total yards? a) 88 b) 188 c) 288

20. Georgia went into the National Championship Game as a favorite by how many points? a) 3 points b) 13 points c) 23 points

Bonus Quiz 3: Answers

1. Ohio State 2. Bulldogs 42-41 Buckeyes 3. Adonai Mitchell 4. Mercedes-Benz Stadium, Atlanta 5. LSU 6. Bulldogs 50-30 Tigers 7. Oregon 8. Vanderbilt 9. True 10. Kenny McIntosh 11. Carson Beck 12. Brock Bowers 13. Kentucky 14. Mykel Williams 15. Christopher Smith 16. False (the winning margin against Missouri was 4 points) 17. Kenny McIntosh, Stetson Bennett and Brock Bowers 18. Third 19. a) 214 points 20. c) 616 points

Bonus Questions Quiz 2: Pot Luck

1. After the 2022 season, Todd Monken left the Bulldogs to become the offensive coordinator of which NFL team?

2. The Philadelphia Eagles used the ninth pick of the 2023 NFL Draft to select which Georgia defensive lineman?

3. Which Bulldog, better known as a receiver, had the longest run during the 2022 season of 75 yards?

4. He scored that 75-yard touchdown in a game against which Mid-American Conference opponent?

5. The longest catch by a Bulldog during the 2022 season was an 83-yard effort courtesy of which running back?

6. Do the Bulldogs have an all-time winning or losing record in Bowl Games?

7. Which team selected quarterback Stetson Bennett in the 2023 NFL Draft?

8. In what round did they make that pick?

9. Immediately prior to being named the offensive coordinator at Georgia in March 2023, Brandon Streeter had been the QBs coach and offensive coordinator at which program?

10. Which all-time Georgia great was given the Contribution to College Football Award by the National College Football Awards Association in 2019?

11. Which NFL team used the 14th pick of the 2023 NFL Draft to select Georgia offensive lineman Broderick Jones?

12. Whose 469 combined rushing and passing yards against Virginia in the 1995 Peach Bowl are the most by a Bulldog in a Bowl Game?

13. Which NFL team selected two Georgia defenders in the first round of the 2022 NFL Draft?

14. Who were those two defenders?

15. Who was the team's leading tackler with 76 tackles during the 2022 National Championship season?

16. Which Bulldog was taken with the first overall pick of the 2022 NFL Draft?

17. Which AFC team made that first overall pick?

18. Whose 266 rushing yards against Louisville in the 2014 Belk Bowl are the most by a Bulldogs rusher in a Bowl Game?

19. Who holds the school record for the longest kickoff return touchdown in a Bowl Game? a) Brandon Boykin b) Reggie Davis c) Isaiah McKenzie

20. Which back holds the record for the longest run by a Bulldogs rusher in a Bowl Game? a) Nick Chubb b) Sony Michel c) Herschel Walker

Bonus Quiz 1: Answers

1. TCU Horned Frogs 2. Georgia 65-7 TCU 3. SoFi Stadium, Los Angeles 4. Stetson Bennett 5. Javon Bullard 6. Branson Robinson and Stetson Bennett 7. Brock Bowers 8. Ladd McConkey 9. Adonai Mitchell 10. True 11. Javon Bullard 12. Brock Bowers 13. Five 14. 38 points 15. Alabama 16. Joe Burrow 17. True 18. Pentatonix 19. b) 188 yards 20. b) 13 points

Bonus Questions Quiz 3: National Champions 2022

1. The Bulldogs reached the National Championship Game after squeaking past which opponent in the semi-final?

2. What was the final score in that epic semi-final?

3. Who caught a 10-yard touchdown pass with less than a minute left in the semi-final?

4. That semi-final was hosted at which stadium?

5. Which opponent did Georgia defeat in the SEC Championship Game?

6. What was the final score in the SEC Championship Game?

7. The Bulldogs opened the season with a 49-3 rout of which #11-ranked PAC-12 school?

8. In week seven the Bulldogs routed which SEC opponent by a score of 55-0?

9. True or false – By the end of the season, the Bulldogs were ranked in the top five nationally in both scoring offense and scoring defense?

10. With 823 yards, who was Georgia's leading rusher in the 2022 season?

11. Stetson Bennett was one of two Bulldogs to throw a touchdown pass in the 2022 season. Who was the other?

12. With 63 catches and 942 yards, who was the leading pass catcher for the Bulldogs in 2022?

13. Only one opponent kept the Bulldogs below 20 points throughout the whole of the season. Which one?

14. Which true freshman led the team in sacks in 2022?

15. Selected by the Las Vegas Raiders in the 2023 NFL Draft, who led the Bulldogs in interceptions in 2022?

16. True or false – The Bulldogs defeated every opponent they faced in 2022 by double digits?

17. Who were the three Bulldogs to score 10 or more touchdowns during the 2022 season?

18. The Bulldogs started the 2022 season ranked at what number in the AP poll?

19. The stingy Bulldogs defense allowed how many points throughout the 2022 season? a) 214 b) 224 c) 234

20. The record-breaking 2022 Bulldogs set a school record for points scored. How many did they amass? a) 596 b) 606 c) 616

Bonus Quiz 2: Answers

1. Baltimore 2. Jalen Carter 3. Brock Bowers 4. Kent State 5. Kenny McIntosh 6. Winning 7. Los Angeles Rams 8. Fourth 9. Clemson 10. Herschel Walker 11. Pittsburgh 12. Santonio Holmes 13. Green Bay 14. Quay Walker and Devonte Wyatt 15. Smael Mondon Jr. 16. Travon Walker 17. Jacksonville 18. Nick Chubb 19. Brandon Boykin 20. b) Sony Michel

9 781916 123090